the King of Shapes!

Ava P. Jones

CONTENTS

Introduction:
Meet Euclid!

Do you love puzzles? The kind of puzzles that make you
stop, scratch your head, and say, "Hmm, how does
this work?" Euclid did too! In fact, Euclid wasn't just
any puzzle lover—he was *the* puzzle master of shapes,
patterns, and math. And he didn't just stop at solving

puzzles; he turned his love for shapes into one of the coolest discoveries ever: the world of geometry!

Let's travel back over 2,000 years ago to meet Euclid, a brilliant thinker whose ideas still shape the way we understand math today. Known as the "father of geometry," Euclid had a knack for asking big questions and finding even bigger answers. He looked at a simple triangle or a straight line and thought, "How does this work? What rules make this so perfect?" Those questions led him to unlock secrets about shapes, patterns, and space that had never been fully explored before.

But Euclid wasn't just a thinker who kept his ideas to himself. He was a teacher, too—a great one! He believed that everyone should be able to understand the magic of geometry, so he wrote a book called *The Elements*. Imagine a guide that explains everything you need to know about shapes and math in a way that's both simple and powerful. That's what *The Elements* was. For centuries, people used it to design towering buildings, create maps of the stars, and even solve everyday problems. It became one of the most famous books in history!

What makes Euclid's story so exciting is that it's not just about math—it's about curiosity and discovery. Euclid wasn't born a genius with all the answers. He started as a kid, just like you, who looked at the world and wondered, "Why?" Why does the moon look round? Why do some rocks stack better than others? Why does a straight line feel so... perfect?

In this book, we're going to follow Euclid's incredible journey. We'll start from his childhood, where his love for shapes began. Then, we'll explore how he grew up in a world filled with knowledge and wonder. We'll dive into the amazing discoveries he made about geometry and see how his ideas changed the world forever. Along the way, you'll get to try out some of Euclid's coolest tricks, spot shapes around you, and maybe even become a geometry master yourself!

Are you ready to step into Euclid's world? A world where triangles tell stories, lines stretch endlessly, and shapes hold secrets waiting to be unlocked? Let's dive in and see what made Euclid the king of shapes. Who knows? You might just find a new way to look at the world, just like he did!

Chapter 1:
A Little Boy with Big Questions

Long before he became known as the "father of geometry," Euclid was just a curious little boy living in the sun-drenched land of Ancient Greece. He didn't have a chalkboard or a math book—those things didn't even exist yet! But what he did have was a sharp mind, a boundless imagination, and a knack for asking the most fascinating questions.

Euclid's home was surrounded by beauty. Picture it: olive trees swayed gently in the breeze, their branches casting lacy shadows on the ground. Beyond the fields, the sparkling blue sea stretched out to meet the horizon, dotted with boats carrying traders from faraway lands. This was the perfect playground for a boy with a curious mind. And Euclid? He never wasted a moment to explore.

"Why is the moon round?" he asked one night, gazing up at the sky. Its silvery glow made him wonder about its perfect shape. "Why does the sun look so small, even though it lights up the whole world?" His questions poured out like water from a fountain, one after another.

By day, he found new puzzles to solve. "Why do rocks
stack better in a pyramid than in a circle?" he
wondered while building towers with pebbles near the
shore. If a stack wobbled and tumbled, Euclid didn't
get frustrated—he got curious. What could he change
to make it stand taller, stronger?

Euclid's family noticed his endless questions, and instead
of brushing them off, they encouraged him to explore.
His father, a merchant who traveled far and wide,

brought back stories of great cities, mighty ships, and even the towering pyramids of Egypt. "They're built so perfectly they've stood for thousands of years," he told Euclid. That simple comment sent the young boy into a daydream about what made the pyramids so strong.

His mother, on the other hand, had a knack for patience. She would smile as Euclid spent hours drawing shapes in the sand with a stick, deep in thought. He'd start with a square, then stretch it into a rectangle. Next, he'd try a triangle. "Why does this one feel so balanced?" he asked, pointing to the triangle, its sharp edges cleanly carved into the sand.

One sunny afternoon, Euclid sat by the sea, letting the waves tickle his toes as he sketched in the sand. A triangle here, a circle there. He drew a straight line and wondered, "How far could this line go if nothing stopped it?" Then he made a curve and compared the two. "Which one is stronger? Which one is faster?"

A seagull squawked above, snapping Euclid out of his thoughts. He looked up and smiled. To him, the world was one giant puzzle, and every pebble, tree, and wave held a piece of the answer.

Euclid's love for shapes didn't stop at the sand. Whenever he visited the marketplace with his family, he was mesmerized by the different patterns. He admired the perfect circles of the pottery, the woven designs of the baskets, and the neat rows of fruit stacked in pyramids. Everything seemed to have its own order, its own set of rules.

At home, Euclid loved to experiment. One day, he tied a piece of string to a stick and spun it in a circle. The string stretched taut, tracing a perfect curve in the dirt. "Is this how the moon moves around the Earth?" he wondered aloud.

His questions often made the adults around him chuckle. "Why do you think about such things, Euclid?" they'd ask. But he didn't mind. For Euclid, every question was like a new adventure, a path that might lead to something amazing.

Even as a child, Euclid had a rare gift: he didn't just see the world as it was—he saw what it could be. A stack of rocks wasn't just a game; it was a lesson in balance. A line wasn't just a mark; it was a doorway to infinity. Every shape, every pattern held a story, and Euclid was determined to uncover them all.

In those early years, no one could have guessed that this curious boy, with sand on his hands and questions in his heart, would one day write a book that would change the world. But if you had asked Euclid? He would have smiled, picked up his stick, and drawn another shape in the sand.

Because to Euclid, the world was a puzzle—and he couldn't wait to solve it.

CHAPTER 2:
THE WONDERS OF ANCIENT ALEXANDRIA

When Euclid arrived in Alexandria, it felt like stepping into a dream. This wasn't just any city—it was one of the most incredible places in the ancient world, a bustling hub of ideas, invention, and inspiration.

Imagine a place where scholars and adventurers from across the globe gathered to share their knowledge. This was Alexandria, a city bursting with the hum of curiosity and discovery.

The streets were alive with activity. Merchants called out their wares in the crowded marketplaces, selling everything from rare spices to scrolls of parchment. Ships sailed into the harbor, their sails billowing in the salty breeze, carrying goods and ideas from faraway lands. Towering over the city was the legendary Lighthouse of Alexandria, its flame guiding sailors safely to shore.

At the heart of it all stood the Library of Alexandria—a place so magnificent it was said to hold all the knowledge of the world. The library wasn't like a library today with shelves of books; it was filled with thousands of scrolls, carefully stored and cataloged.

Scholars wandered the halls, debating, writing, and dreaming up new ideas.

When Euclid first walked through the library's grand doors, he was awestruck. The sight of scrolls stacked from floor to ceiling made his heart race. Here were answers to questions he had never even thought to ask. Astronomy, medicine, poetry, mathematics—it was all here, waiting to be discovered.

But Alexandria wasn't just about the library. It was home to brilliant teachers and eager students, all part of a vibrant learning community. Euclid soon found himself among peers who shared his love for knowledge. They spent hours discussing the mysteries of the universe, challenging each other's ideas and learning from one another.

Euclid's favorite teacher was a wise and patient mathematician named Ptolemy. Ptolemy loved asking questions just as much as Euclid did. One day, he posed a riddle to the class: "If a triangle's angles always add up to the same amount, why is that number so important?"

Euclid's mind buzzed with possibilities. He thought about the shapes he used to draw in the sand, the patterns he saw in the marketplace, and the perfect balance of triangles. He didn't know the answer right away, but he was excited to figure it out.

Euclid soon discovered that studying in Alexandria wasn't always easy. The city was full of distractions—festivals, bustling markets, and the constant arrival of travelers with stories of adventure. Plus, the scrolls in the library were written in dense, complicated language, making them tough to understand.

One day, Euclid faced his biggest challenge yet. He stumbled upon a scroll that described a strange new idea about shapes and numbers. The scroll was filled with diagrams and symbols he had never seen before. At first, it felt like trying to solve a puzzle with missing pieces.

Frustrated but determined, Euclid spent days poring over the scroll. He sketched shapes, measured angles, and scribbled notes, trying to make sense of it all. His classmates teased him for working so hard, saying, "Give it up, Euclid! No one understands that old scroll." But Euclid refused to quit.

Finally, after what felt like an eternity, something clicked. The diagrams and symbols began to make sense. Euclid realized the scroll was describing a rule about triangles, a rule that could be applied to other shapes, too. The discovery filled him with joy.

He rushed to Ptolemy to share what he had learned. "Ah, Euclid," his teacher said with a smile. "Now you see the beauty of perseverance. Math isn't about getting the answers quickly—it's about the journey of understanding."

From that day forward, Euclid became known as the student who never gave up. His love for solving problems, no matter how tough, inspired his classmates. They began to see math not as a chore, but as a way to explore the world's secrets.

Living in Alexandria changed Euclid forever. The city's energy, its treasure trove of knowledge, and its community of thinkers fueled his imagination. Every scroll he read, every conversation he had, and every challenge he faced brought him closer to the groundbreaking ideas he would one day share with the world.

For Euclid, Alexandria wasn't just a city. It was a place where his curiosity could grow, where questions led to discoveries, and where the impossible suddenly seemed possible.

CHAPTER 3:
CRACKING THE PUZZLE OF
SHAPES

Euclid's fascination with shapes was unstoppable. Every time he looked around, he saw the world through a lens of lines, curves, and patterns. While others might pass by a simple triangle or a circle without a second thought, Euclid saw a puzzle waiting to be solved. What made these shapes work the way they did? Why did they seem so perfect, so balanced?

To Euclid, shapes were like a secret language, and he was determined to learn how to read it.

One sunny afternoon, as he strolled through Alexandria, Euclid started noticing shapes everywhere. The fruit stalls in the market were filled with rows of oranges—

each a perfect sphere. The rooftops of homes formed neat triangles, and the woven mats on the ground were made of squares and rectangles. Even the wheels of carts, worn smooth from travel, formed precise circles.

"Shapes are everywhere," Euclid thought to himself. "But why do they look so different? Why are circles so smooth and triangles so pointy? What makes them special?"

These questions buzzed in his mind as he made his way back to his workshop. His workshop wasn't grand— it was just a small space with a wooden table, a few tools, and piles of parchment for drawing. But for Euclid, it was the perfect place to tinker, experiment, and explore.

One day, Euclid decided to experiment with clay. He rolled it into a smooth ball, pressing and shaping it until it was as round as he could make it. Then, with a flat board, he carefully pressed the ball until it formed a flat, round disk. "A perfect circle," he whispered, marveling at the smooth curve.

But Euclid didn't stop there. He flattened the clay further and cut it into a square. Then he made a triangle. Each shape had its own personality. The square, with its even sides and sharp corners, felt sturdy and balanced.

The triangle seemed sharp and dynamic, like it was always ready to point somewhere. The circle was soft, smooth, and endless—it had no corners, no edges, just one continuous curve.

"What makes these shapes so different?" Euclid asked himself. "And why does each one feel special in its own way?"

To test his ideas, Euclid began building simple models out of wood. He carved small triangles, rectangles, and circles and started playing with them. He stacked them, fitted them together, and even tried balancing them. He noticed that triangles were surprisingly strong, even when stacked at odd angles. Squares fit together perfectly, leaving no gaps. And circles? They could roll!

One day, Euclid's friend, a carpenter named Aesop, stopped by to visit. "What are you working on, Euclid?" Aesop asked, watching him balance a wooden triangle on its tip.

"Shapes," Euclid replied, his eyes gleaming with excitement. "Look at this triangle. It doesn't wobble, no matter how I place it. But this square? It needs a flat surface to stay steady."

Aesop nodded thoughtfully. "That's why we use triangles to make sturdy roofs," he said. "They don't collapse under weight."

"Exactly!" Euclid exclaimed. "Triangles are strong because their sides lock together. And look at this circle." He rolled the wooden disk across the table. "It's perfect for wheels. No bumps, no edges, just smooth motion."

Aesop laughed. "Leave it to you, Euclid, to find the magic in a piece of wood."

As Euclid continued his experiments, he began to notice patterns and relationships between shapes. He discovered that if you add up the angles of a triangle, they always equal the same amount—no matter how big or small the triangle is. He found that squares could be divided into triangles and that circles had mysterious properties that made them endlessly fascinating.

Each discovery felt like unlocking a new piece of the puzzle. Euclid realized that these weren't just random coincidences—there were rules guiding the way shapes worked.

One evening, as he sat under the stars, Euclid thought about his experiments with clay and wood. He wondered if these same rules applied to the world around him. "If shapes follow patterns," he mused, "then maybe everything does. The stars, the Earth, even the way we build our homes—they all have rules waiting to be discovered."

With every new insight, Euclid's love for geometry grew deeper. To him, shapes weren't just objects—they were the building blocks of the universe. Circles, triangles, and squares weren't just pretty to look at; they held secrets about how the world worked.

But Euclid wasn't content to keep these discoveries to himself. He wanted to share them with others, to show them how shapes and patterns could explain so many things in life. He dreamed of a way to teach these ideas so that anyone—whether a carpenter like Aesop or a young student—could understand and use them.

This dream would eventually lead him to write *The Elements,* a book that would change the world. But

33

for now, Euclid was just a curious thinker, cracking the puzzle of shapes one question at a time.

CHAPTER 4:
THE MAKING OF *THE*
ELEMENTS

By the time Euclid decided to write *The Elements,* he had spent years exploring shapes, patterns, and the rules of geometry. He had tested ideas, solved puzzles, and uncovered secrets about the way the world worked. But he wasn't just interested in knowing these things for himself—Euclid wanted to share his discoveries with everyone.

That's how *The Elements,* one of the most important books in history, was born.

At its heart, *The Elements* was like an instruction manual for understanding geometry. Euclid didn't just present a bunch of random facts about shapes and angles. Instead, he carefully organized his discoveries into a step-by-step guide, starting with the simplest ideas and building up to the more complex ones. It was as if he were teaching readers how to build a house, one brick at a time.

"First, let's lay the foundation," Euclid might have said. He began with basic definitions, like what a point is ("a location with no size") and what a line is ("a straight path that goes on forever"). These were the simplest ideas—the bricks at the very bottom of the house.

Next, Euclid added more layers. He explained how to connect points to make lines and how to combine lines to create shapes like triangles, squares, and circles. Each rule built on the last, like stacking bricks higher and higher. By the end of the book, Euclid had created an entire structure of knowledge, showing how everything in geometry fit together perfectly.

What made *The Elements* so special wasn't just its content—it was how Euclid wrote it. He didn't just tell people what to believe. Instead, he proved every idea step by step, using logic and reasoning. It was like solving a mystery, where every clue led to the next big discovery.

Imagine opening *The Elements* and finding a challenge: "Prove that the angles of a triangle always add up to the same amount." Euclid wouldn't just give you the answer. He'd guide you through the steps to figure it out yourself. His book wasn't just about learning facts—it was about teaching people how to think.

But *The Elements* wasn't just for students in a classroom. Its ideas had a huge impact on the real world. Builders and architects used Euclid's rules to design temples, roads, and aqueducts that stood tall and strong. The great pyramids of Egypt—some of the most impressive structures ever built—relied on the principles of geometry.

Even sailors used geometry to navigate the seas. They calculated angles and distances to figure out their location, making sure they could sail from one port to another safely. Without geometry, entire cities couldn't have been built, and explorers might never have found their way home.

What's amazing is that *The Elements* wasn't just useful in Euclid's time—it's still important today. Over 2,000 years later, people are still studying his work. From designing skyscrapers to creating computer graphics, the rules in *The Elements* are everywhere.

But how did Euclid manage to write a book so timeless and brilliant? The answer lies in his unique way of thinking. Euclid believed that the simplest ideas could lead to the most powerful discoveries. He wasn't interested in shortcuts or quick answers. Instead, he focused on understanding things deeply and showing others how to do the same.

Writing *The Elements* wasn't easy. It took time, patience, and a lot of hard work. Euclid had to organize his thoughts, draw clear diagrams, and make sure every rule made sense. But he loved the process, because he knew it would help others see the beauty of geometry.

When Euclid finally completed *The Elements,* he didn't expect fame or fortune. He simply wanted to share what he had learned. But his book became so popular that it spread far and wide, copied by scribes and studied by scholars across the ancient world. It became the go-to guide for anyone who wanted to understand geometry, earning Euclid the title of "the father of geometry."

To Euclid, *The Elements* wasn't just a book—it was a way to share the magic of shapes and patterns with everyone. And for thousands of years, it has done exactly that.

Chapter 5:
Cool Geometry Tricks!

Euclid didn't just write *The Elements* to be a dense book of rules and theorems—he wanted to share the *fun* of geometry. To him, shapes and lines weren't just things you saw on paper or in the sand; they were the building blocks of the world, and they came with some pretty amazing tricks. Let's take a look at a few of Euclid's coolest ideas—simple yet mind-blowing concepts that you can see in action everywhere!

The Shortest Path Between Two Points

Imagine you're standing at one side of a park, and your favorite ice cream truck is at the other. What's the fastest way to get there? You might zigzag around trees or wander along the park's paths, but Euclid had a much simpler answer: the shortest path between two points is a straight line.

It seems obvious now, right? But over 2,000 years ago, no one had thought to put this idea into words the way Euclid did. He proved it in *The Elements* using logic and simple diagrams. Euclid showed that if you take any two points—let's call them A and B—and draw a straight line connecting them, that line will always be the shortest possible route.

But here's where it gets fun: you can test this yourself! Grab a piece of string and two pins. Stick the pins into a board at two different points, and stretch the string tightly between them. What do you see? A perfectly straight line! No matter how you stretch the string, it will always follow the shortest path.

Euclid's rule is more than just a fun experiment—it's used all the time in the real world. Architects use it to design buildings, engineers use it to plan roads, and even delivery drivers use it to figure out the fastest route to your house. Next time you're heading somewhere, think about Euclid's trick: the shortest path is always straight ahead!

All Right Angles Are Equal

Now, let's talk about right angles. You've probably seen them a million times—on the corners of books, windows, or even the screen of your tablet. But did you know that all right angles are *exactly* the same?

Euclid thought this was fascinating. He defined a right angle as the perfect 90-degree corner, where two lines meet to form a square corner. What's amazing is that no matter how big or small your lines are, if they form a right angle, it's always equal to every other right angle in the world.

Here's an experiment to try: take a sheet of paper and fold one corner until it forms a sharp square edge. That's your right angle! Now compare it to the corners of different objects around you—a book, a picture frame, or the tiles on the floor. They all match perfectly.

Why does this matter? Well, without right angles, we wouldn't have many of the things we use every day. Houses, tables, computers, and even soccer fields rely on the precision of right angles to stay strong and functional. Thanks to Euclid's trick, builders and designers know their corners will always line up, no matter where they're working.

Circles: The Shape That Keeps Going

Let's not forget one of Euclid's favorite shapes: the circle. Euclid loved circles because they were so simple yet so full of surprises. He discovered that every circle has a center point, and every point along the edge of the circle is exactly the same distance from the center. This distance is called the radius, and it's one of the keys to understanding how circles work.

Think about a wheel on a bike. It spins perfectly because every part of the wheel is the same distance from its center. That's Euclid's rule in action! Without it, we wouldn't have smooth wheels, round tables, or even basketballs that bounce evenly.

Here's a fun fact: Euclid also figured out how to draw a perfect circle. All you need is a stick, a piece of string, and something to mark the ground with, like chalk. Tie one end of the string to the stick, hold the other end taut, and spin around in a circle. Presto! You've just made a shape as perfect as anything Euclid could draw.

Euclid's Tricks Are Everywhere

What makes Euclid's ideas so cool is that they aren't just limited to math class—they're everywhere!

In sports: The shortest path rule helps soccer players pass the ball as quickly as possible.

In art: Right angles are used to frame pictures and create sculptures.

In technology: Circles and lines are essential for designing everything from wheels to smartphones.

Euclid's geometry might be ancient, but it's far from outdated. Every time you see a triangle, a rectangle, or a perfect circle, you're looking at shapes that follow the same rules Euclid discovered thousands of years ago.

So, next time you pick up a ruler or start doodling shapes, remember Euclid's tricks. With just a few simple ideas, he unlocked the secrets of the world—and you can, too!

Chapter 6:
The World's First Math Superstar

Today, we think of celebrities as actors, athletes, or musicians—but over 2,000 years ago, there was a different kind of star: Euclid. Long before Instagram or YouTube, Euclid became famous for something that might surprise you—math! His brilliant ideas, clear teaching, and groundbreaking book *The Elements* turned him into one of the most respected scholars of his time. People from all over the ancient world came to Alexandria just to learn from him, making Euclid one of history's very first math superstars.

A Teacher Like No Other

Euclid wasn't just a genius mathematician—he was also a
    fantastic teacher. He had a way of explaining even the
    trickiest ideas so that his students could understand
    them. Instead of simply handing out answers, Euclid
    guided his students to discover the answers for
    themselves. He believed that learning wasn't about
    memorizing facts; it was about understanding *why*
    those facts were true.

Euclid's classroom in Alexandria was always buzzing with excitement. His students came from all walks of life: young scholars hoping to become the next great mathematicians, architects eager to design stronger buildings, and even curious travelers who had heard of Euclid's reputation and wanted to see what all the fuss was about.

One day, during a lesson about triangles, a particularly impatient student raised his hand. "Master Euclid," the student asked, "why are we learning all of this? What's the point of geometry?"

Euclid paused, a small smile forming on his face. "Ah," he said, "so you want to know why math is important?"

The student nodded eagerly.

Euclid walked over to the student's desk and handed him a small coin. "Take this," Euclid said. "It is your reward for asking such a question."

The student looked confused. "A reward?"

"Yes," Euclid replied. "If you believe you need a reward for learning, then take it. But remember this: math is its own reward."

The classroom fell silent as the students considered Euclid's words. What did he mean by that? Over time, they began to understand. Math wasn't just about solving problems or finding answers—it was about the joy of discovery, the thrill of understanding something new, and the power to see the world in a different way.

A Star in Alexandria

Word of Euclid's teaching spread far and wide. Scholars and students traveled great distances to study with him in Alexandria. Some came from Greece, others from Egypt, and some even from distant lands like Persia and India. They all wanted to learn the secrets of geometry from the man who had unlocked its mysteries.

Euclid's fame grew not because he sought it, but because of the incredible impact of his work. His book *The Elements* was already becoming a must-read for anyone interested in mathematics, but seeing Euclid teach in person was a whole different experience. He made math come alive, showing how shapes, lines, and patterns weren't just abstract ideas but tools for understanding the world.

Imagine being one of Euclid's students, sitting in his classroom as he sketched shapes on a piece of parchment. He'd draw a perfect circle and explain how every point along its edge was the same distance from the center. Then he'd challenge the class: "Why is this important? How can you use this knowledge in the real world?"

At first, the answers didn't always come easily. But with Euclid's guidance, his students began to see how geometry could solve problems, build stronger structures, and even help map the stars. They realized they weren't just learning math—they were learning to think like problem-solvers.

Math's First Superstar

Euclid's fame wasn't like that of a modern-day celebrity, with crowds cheering and people asking for autographs. Instead, his influence was quieter but no less powerful. People admired him not for how he looked or what he wore, but for his ideas and the way he changed their understanding of the world.

In many ways, Euclid was the first "math star." His work inspired countless scholars to follow in his footsteps, and his teachings became the foundation for future discoveries in science, engineering, and architecture. Even today, his name is known by anyone who studies geometry.

But what made Euclid truly remarkable was that he didn't care about fame or recognition. For him, the reward wasn't in being celebrated—it was in knowing that his ideas could help others learn, grow, and see the beauty of math.

So the next time you sit down to solve a tricky problem or work on a math puzzle, remember Euclid—the world's first math superstar, a teacher who believed that math wasn't just useful, but magical.

CHAPTER 7:
EUCLID'S GEOMETRY AROUND
THE GLOBE

Euclid's ideas didn't stay in Alexandria. They spread far and wide, traveling across oceans, over mountains, and through centuries. His book, *The Elements*, was like a tiny pebble dropped into a pond, sending ripples of knowledge across the entire world. People from all walks of life found ways to use his discoveries, and his geometry became one of the most important tools for shaping the future.

Roman Architects: Building the Ancient World

The Romans were some of the first to take Euclid's ideas and put them into action. They were master builders, famous for their grand temples, towering aqueducts, and massive stadiums like the Colosseum. But without geometry, none of these structures would have been possible.

Roman architects relied on Euclid's rules to measure angles, calculate distances, and ensure their buildings were strong and stable. For example, when they built arches—one of their signature designs—they used Euclid's understanding of circles to get the curves just right. The result? Structures that could support massive amounts of weight and still stand tall thousands of years later.

Even today, when you walk through ancient Roman ruins, you're seeing Euclid's geometry in action. Those perfect columns, symmetrical designs, and intricate mosaics owe their existence to the math he discovered.

Sailors: Navigating the Open Seas

Long before GPS and smartphones, sailors had to rely on the stars, maps, and geometry to find their way. Euclid's work played a huge role in helping explorers navigate the open seas. His rules about angles and lines were essential for creating accurate maps and measuring distances.

For example, when a sailor wanted to figure out how far they were from land, they would use a device called an astrolabe. This tool, based on geometric principles, helped them measure the angle of a star above the horizon. By combining this information with Euclid's math, sailors could estimate their position and steer their ships in the right direction.

Thanks to Euclid, sailors weren't just guessing their way across the ocean—they were using geometry to travel farther than ever before. His ideas helped them explore new lands, trade goods, and connect the world in ways that had never been imagined.

Astronauts: Exploring the Final Frontier

Euclid's geometry isn't just useful on Earth—it's essential for exploring outer space too! Astronauts and scientists use the same rules of lines, angles, and shapes to design rockets, map the stars, and even calculate the best way to land on distant planets.

For example, when NASA sends a spacecraft to Mars, they use geometry to figure out the best path for the journey. They calculate the angles of the rocket's trajectory, the curvature of the planet's surface, and the distance between Earth and Mars—all using principles that Euclid first wrote about in *The Elements*.

It's amazing to think that the same math Euclid used to draw shapes in the sand is now helping humans reach the stars.

Euclid's Geometry in Modern Life

Even if you're not building temples, sailing the seas, or exploring space, you've probably used Euclid's geometry without even realizing it.

Video Games: Game developers use geometry to create virtual worlds. Every 3D character, mountain, or building in a video game is made up of geometric shapes, carefully designed to look realistic and move smoothly.

Bridges: Engineers use Euclid's principles to design bridges that are strong enough to support heavy traffic while staying balanced and secure. Have you ever noticed how many bridges are made of triangles?

That's because triangles are one of the strongest shapes in geometry, something Euclid explained over 2,000 years ago.

Art: Artists use geometry to create beautiful works of art, from perfectly symmetrical paintings to sculptures that play with shapes and patterns. Even the famous Leonardo da Vinci studied Euclid's work to improve his designs.

A Universal Language

What makes Euclid's geometry so incredible is that it doesn't matter where you're from or what language you speak—his ideas are universal. A triangle is a triangle, whether you're in Ancient Rome, modern-day America, or on a spaceship heading to Mars. His rules connect people across time and space, showing us that math truly is the language of the universe.

Thanks to Euclid, we've been able to design towering skyscrapers, map the stars, and create technologies that seemed impossible just a century ago. His geometry is everywhere, shaping our world in ways big and small.

The next time you walk across a bridge, play a video game, or gaze up at the night sky, take a moment to think about Euclid. His ideas traveled around the globe—and even beyond—proving that one person's discoveries can truly change the world.

CHAPTER 8:
THE MYSTERY OF EUCLID

For someone as famous as Euclid, you might expect there to be stories about his life—where he was born, what he liked to eat, or how he spent his days. But here's the surprising thing: we know very little about Euclid as a person.

Unlike kings, warriors, or poets of his time, Euclid didn't leave behind letters, speeches, or portraits. No statues were built in his honor, and no one wrote down stories about him. In fact, most of what we know about him comes from his incredible work, *The Elements*. It's almost as if Euclid didn't want people to remember him—he just wanted them to remember his ideas.

A Scholar Who Loved His Work

Historians believe Euclid lived around 300 BCE in Alexandria, Egypt, but we don't know exactly when he was born or when he died. Some say he was originally from Greece and moved to Alexandria to study and teach. Others think he might have been a local who grew up surrounded by the city's culture of learning.

What we do know is that Euclid was a dedicated scholar. He spent most of his life studying, teaching, and writing about math. He didn't care about fame or fortune—his greatest joy came from solving puzzles, discovering new ideas, and sharing his knowledge with others.

Imagine what Euclid's life might have been like. He probably started his day early, working in a quiet study filled with scrolls, ink, and rulers. His desk might have been cluttered with sketches of triangles, circles, and other shapes, each one a step closer to uncovering a new rule of geometry.

In the afternoons, Euclid likely taught his students, using simple tools like string, sticks, and sand to explain complex ideas. He didn't have fancy technology or textbooks—just his sharp mind and his love for math.

At night, under the flickering light of an oil lamp, Euclid might have worked on *The Elements*, carefully organizing his thoughts and drawing diagrams. He wasn't writing for fame or recognition—he was writing to preserve knowledge and make it accessible to others.

The Legend of Euclid

Over the centuries, Euclid became more than just a person—he became a legend. Stories about him were passed down through generations, often blending fact with imagination. One famous tale describes a student asking Euclid for a shortcut to learn geometry. Euclid replied, "There is no royal road to geometry," meaning there are no shortcuts—you have to put in the work to truly understand.

This story shows us how much Euclid valued learning for its own sake. He believed that understanding math was its own reward, a lesson that still inspires students today.

Why the Mystery?

So, why didn't Euclid leave behind more clues about his life? The answer might be simple: he didn't think his personal story was important.

For Euclid, the ideas were what mattered most. He wasn't interested in being remembered as a famous scholar— he wanted his work to speak for itself. And it did. *The Elements* became one of the most influential books in history, studied by mathematicians, scientists, and thinkers for over 2,000 years.

In a way, the mystery of Euclid adds to his brilliance. He reminds us that great discoveries don't always need a famous name attached to them. Sometimes, the work itself is the real star.

A Quiet Genius

If Euclid could see how his ideas have shaped the world, he might smile quietly and return to his work. He wasn't someone who sought applause or recognition. He was a thinker, a problem-solver, and a teacher who believed in the power of knowledge.

Perhaps that's the greatest mystery of all: how a man we know so little about could leave behind ideas that changed the world forever.

Chapter 9:
What We Can Learn from Euclid

Euclid lived over 2,000 years ago, but his story is still inspiring people today. Why? Because he wasn't just a mathematician—he was a thinker, a problem-solver, and a teacher who showed us how powerful curiosity and determination can be.

Even if you've never drawn a triangle or measured an angle, there's so much we can learn from Euclid's life. His lessons go beyond math—they're about how we approach the world, solve problems, and chase our dreams. Let's explore some of the most important things Euclid teaches us.

Curiosity Drives Discovery

Euclid's journey began with a simple thing: questions. As a child, he asked why the moon was round, why rocks stacked better in pyramids, and what made shapes so special. He didn't settle for easy answers—he wanted to dig deeper and uncover the truth.

That curiosity led him to study shapes, patterns, and rules. Over time, it helped him discover new ideas that no one had ever thought of before.

What's amazing is that curiosity isn't just something Euclid had—it's something all of us have. Think about the last time you asked "why" or "how." Maybe you wondered how birds fly, why plants grow, or what makes a rainbow. Those questions are the start of discovery, just like they were for Euclid.

So, never stop asking questions. Whether it's about math, science, art, or the world around you, curiosity can lead you to incredible places.

Patience and Persistence Pay Off

Euclid didn't make his discoveries overnight. He spent years testing ideas, solving problems, and writing *The Elements*. Along the way, he faced challenges—scrolls that were hard to read, problems that seemed impossible to solve, and students who doubted the importance of geometry.

But Euclid didn't give up. He kept working, kept learning, and kept exploring until he found answers. His patience and persistence are a big part of why we remember him today.

The truth is, anything worth doing takes time and effort. Whether you're learning to ride a bike, play an instrument, or solve a math problem, there will be moments when it feels hard. But just like Euclid, you can overcome those challenges with patience and determination.

Here's a trick: the next time you feel stuck, take a deep breath and remind yourself that even the greatest minds—like Euclid—faced tough moments. Keep going, and you might just surprise yourself with what you can achieve.

One Person's Ideas Can Shape the World

Euclid didn't know how far his ideas would travel. He didn't set out to become famous or change the course of history. He simply wanted to share what he had discovered about shapes and geometry.

But those ideas went on to shape the world in incredible ways. They helped build ancient temples, map the

78

stars, and even send rockets into space. Euclid's work shows us that one person's ideas—no matter how small they seem at first—can make a big difference.

And that means *your* ideas can make a difference too. Whether you dream of inventing something new, writing a story, or solving a problem, your unique perspective matters. Just like Euclid, you have the power to change the world in ways you can't even imagine yet.

Follow Your Own Questions

Euclid didn't follow a straight path in life—he followed his questions. He explored the things that fascinated him, from triangles and circles to the rules of geometry. That's what made his work so special.

You can do the same! Think about what excites you. Maybe it's building things, drawing, writing, or exploring nature. Whatever it is, dive into it with curiosity and enthusiasm. Ask questions, try new things, and don't be afraid to make mistakes along the way.

Euclid's story teaches us that it's okay to go at your own pace and follow your unique interests. The world is full of possibilities, and your curiosity can lead you to amazing discoveries.

A Legacy of Learning

Euclid's life reminds us that learning is a lifelong journey. It's not about getting all the answers right—it's about exploring, growing, and discovering something new every day.

So the next time you face a challenge or wonder about something, think of Euclid. His curiosity, patience, and persistence changed the world—and yours can too.

Chapter 10:
Shapes Everywhere!

Look around you—what do you see? Maybe you're sitting at a table with a rectangle for its top, or glancing out a window framed by perfect right angles. Perhaps there's a clock nearby with its circular face ticking away the time. Everywhere you look, Euclid's geometry is hiding in plain sight!

Euclid's discoveries aren't just stuck in ancient books or classrooms—they're part of our everyday lives. Triangles, circles, squares, and lines are everywhere, shaping the world around us. The bridges we cross, the games we play, and even the buildings we live in all rely on the rules Euclid discovered over 2,000 years ago.

Here's a fun challenge: the next time you step outside, try to find as many shapes as you can. Look for triangles in rooftops, circles in car wheels, and rectangles in street signs. Can you spot any patterns? Count the shapes around you, and imagine how Euclid might have studied them.

Remember, Euclid started just like you—with a curious mind and a love for discovery. So the next time you see a triangle or a circle, take a moment to think of him—

the kid who turned shapes into magic and showed us that math is everywhere.

FREE Audio Bonus

Kindly Scan the Code to get the Audio Version of this book for FREE.

Other Books by the Author:

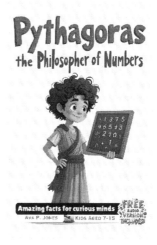

Made in the USA
Middletown, DE
11 June 2025